Level

Butterfly Lovers

梁山伯与祝英台

王亚西 改编

MP3
Download Online
www.sinolingua.com.cn

SINOLINGUA
华语教学出版社

First Edition 2016
Second Printing 2017

ISBN 978-7-5138-0975-7
Copyright 2016 by Sinolingua Co., Ltd
Published by Sinolingua Co., Ltd
24 Baiwanzhuang Road, Beijing 100037, China
Tel: (86) 10-68320585 68997826
Fax: (86) 10-68997826 68326333
http://www.sinolingua.com.cn
E-mail: hyjx@sinolingua.com.cn
Facebook: www.facebook.com/sinolingua
Printed by Beijing Xicheng Printing Co., Ltd

Printed in the People's Republic of China

编者的话

对于广大汉语学习者来说，要想快速提高汉语水平，扩大阅读量是很有必要的。"彩虹桥"汉语分级读物为汉语学习者提供了一系列有趣、有用的汉语阅读材料。本系列读物按照词汇量进行分级，力求用限定的词汇讲述精彩的故事。本套读物主要有以下特点：

一、分级精准，循序渐进。我们参考"新汉语水平考试（HSK）词汇表"（2012 年修订版）、《汉语国际教育用音节汉字词汇等级划分（国家标准）》和《常用汉语 1500 高频词语表》等词汇分级标准，结合《欧洲语言教学与评估框架性共同标准》（CEFR），设计了一套适合汉语学习者的"彩虹桥"词汇分级标准。本系列读物分为 7 个级别（入门级*、1 级、2 级、3 级、4 级、5 级、6 级），供不同水平的汉语学习者选择，每个级别故事的生词数量不超过本级别对应词汇量的 20%。随着级别的升高，故事的篇幅逐渐加长。本系列读物与 HSK、CEFR 的对应级别，各级词汇量以及每本书的字数详见下表。

---

* 入门级（Starter）在封底用 S 标识。

级别	入门级	1级	2级	3级	4级	5级	6级
对应级别	HSK1 CEFR A1	HSK1-2 CEFR A1-A2	HSK2-3 CEFR A2-B1	HSK3 CEFR A2-B1	HSK3-4 CEFR B1	HSK4 CEFR B1-B2	HSK5 CEFR B2-C1
词汇量	150	300	500	750	1 000	1 500	2 500
字数	1 000	2 500	5 000	7 500	10 000	15 000	25 000

二、**故事精彩，题材多样**。本套读物选材的标准就是"精彩"，所选的故事要么曲折离奇，要么感人至深，对读者构成奇妙的吸引力。选题广泛取材于中国的神话传说、民间故事、文学名著、名人传记和历史故事等，让汉语学习者在阅读中潜移默化地了解中国的文化和历史。

三、**结构合理，实用性强**。"彩虹桥"系列读物的每一本书中，除了中文故事正文之外，都配有主要人物的中英文介绍、生词英文注释及例句、故事正文的英文翻译、练习题和生词表，方便读者阅读和理解故事内容，提升汉语阅读能力。练习题主要采用客观题，题型多样，难度适中，并附有参考答案，既可供汉语教师在课堂上教学使用，又可供汉语学习者进行自我水平检测。

如果您对本系列读物有什么想法，比如推荐精彩故事、提出改进意见等，请发邮件到 liuxiaolin@sinolingua.com.cn，与我们交流探讨。也可以关注我们的微信公众号 CHQRainbowBridge，随时与我们交流互动。同时，微信公众号会不定期发布有关"彩虹桥"的出版信息，以及汉语阅读、中国文化小知识等。

韩　颖　刘小琳

Preface

For students who study Chinese as a foreign language, it's crucial for them to enlarge the scope of their reading to improve their comprehension skills. The "Rainbow Bridge" Graded Chinese Reader series is designed to provide a collection of interesting and useful Chinese reading materials. This series grades each volume by its vocabulary level and brings the learners into every scene through vivid storytelling. The series has the following features:

I. A gradual approach by grading the volumes based on vocabulary levels. We have consulted the New HSK Vocabulary (2012 Revised Edition), the *Graded Chinese Syllables, Characters and Words for the Application of Teaching Chinese to the Speakers of Other Languages (National Standard)* and the 1500 Commonly Used High Frequency Chinese Vocabulary, along with the Common European Framework of Reference for Languages (CEFR) to design the "Rainbow Bridge" vocabulary grading standard. The series is divided into seven levels (Starter*, Level 1, Level 2, Level 3, Level 4, Level 5 and Level 6) for students at different stages in their Chinese education to choose from. For each level, new words are no more than 20% of the vocabulary amount as specified in the corresponding HSK and CEFR levels.

---

* Represented by "S" on the back cover.

As the levels progress, the passage length will in turn increase. The following table indicates the corresponding "Rainbow Bridge" level, HSK and CEFR levels, the vocabulary amount, and number of characters.

Level	Starter	1	2	3	4	5	6
HSK/ CEFR Level	HSK1 CEFR A1	HSK1-2 CEFR A1-A2	HSK2-3 CEFR A2-B1	HSK3 CEFR A2-B1	HSK3-4 CEFR B1	HSK4 CEFR B1-B2	HSK5 CEFR B2-C1
Vocabulary	150	300	500	750	1,000	1,500	2,500
Characters	1,000	2,500	5,000	7,500	10,000	15,000	25,000

II. Intriguing stories on various themes. The series features engaging stories known for their twists and turns as well as deeply touching plots. The readers will find it a joyful experience to read the stories. The topics are selected from Chinese mythology, legends, folklore, literary classics, biographies of renowned people and historical tales. Such widely ranged topics would exert an invisible, yet formative, influence on readers' understanding of Chinese culture and history.

III. Reasonably structured and easy to use. For each volume of the "Rainbow Bridge" series, apart from a Chinese story, we also provide an introduction to the main characters in Chinese and English, new words with English explanations and sample sentences, and an English translation of the story, followed by comprehension exercises and a vocabulary list to help users read and understand the story and improve their Chinese reading skills. The exercises are mainly presented as objective questions that take on various forms with moderate difficulty. Moreover, keys to the exercises are also provided. The series can be used by teachers in class or by students for self-study.

If you have any questions, comments or suggestions about the series, please email us at liuxiaolin@sinolingua.com.cn. You can also exchange ideas with us via our WeChat account: CHQRainbowBridge. This account will provide updates on the series along with Chinese reading materials and cultural tips.

Han Ying and Liu Xiaolin

主要人物介绍
Main Characters in the Story

梁山伯 (Liáng Shānbó)：男，祝英台的同学和恋人。
Liang Shanbo: Male, Zhu Yingtai's classmate and love.

祝英台 (Zhù Yīngtái)：女，梁山伯的同学和恋人。
Zhu Yingtai: Female, Liang Shanbo's classmate and love.

祝员外 (Zhù Yuánwài)：祝英台的父亲。
Squire Zhu: Zhu Yingtai's father.

银　心 (Yínxīn)：祝英台的丫环。
Yinxin: Zhu Yingtai's servant girl.

四　九 (Sìjiǔ)：梁山伯的书童。
Sijiu: Liang Shanbo's servant boy attending to his study.

马文才 (Mǎ Wéncái)：一位有钱人家的儿子，祝英台的父亲做主，想要她嫁的人。
Ma Wencai: The son of a wealthy family whom Zhu Yingtai's father forced her to marry.

梁山伯与祝英台

① 聪明 (cōngmíng)
adj. clever, intelligent
e.g., 这个女孩儿很
聪明，一学就会。

从前有个姓祝的有钱人，大家都叫他祝员外，他有一个女儿叫祝英台。祝英台不仅长得漂亮，而且还很聪明①。她很喜欢读书写字，但是那时候，女孩子是不能出去上学读书的。英台每天坐在自己房

1

间的窗户①旁边，望着外面来来往往的读书人，她的心早就飞出去了。

英台想，女孩子难道就真的只能每天关在家里吗？我为什么不能出去上学呢？她把丫环②银心叫过来，一起想出了一个好办法③：打扮④成男孩子的样子去外地上学。

① 窗户 (chuānghu) *n.* window
e.g., 这个房间有一个很大的窗户，所以很明亮。

② 丫环 (yāhuan) *n.* maid, servant girl
e.g., 过去，中国富人家的小姐都有丫环伺候。

③ 办法 (bànfǎ) *n.* method, means, way
e.g., 我想出了一个好办法。

④ 打扮 (dǎban) *v.* dress up, make up
e.g., 女孩子都喜欢打扮得漂漂亮亮的。

① 书童 (shūtóng) *n.*
servant boy attend-
ing to study
e.g., 过去, 中国富人
家的男孩儿都有书童
陪他读书。

② 大厅 (dàtīng) *n.*
hall, lobby
e.g., 他家有一个很大
的大厅, 可以举行舞
会。

　　这一天, 祝英台把自己打扮成一个男子, 把丫环银心打扮成她的书童①, 去见她的父母。这时, 英台的父亲和母亲正在大厅②里喝茶, 忽然看到一个男子带着一个书童进来, 向他们问好, 她的父母马上站起来回答, 还请问这个男子的姓名。

祝英台看到父母都没有认①出她来，心里非常高兴。她脱②下男孩子的衣服，现出她本来的样子，再次向父母问好。父母这才发现原来是自己的女儿。父亲生气地说："女孩子就应该像个女孩子的样子，

① 认（出）[rèn(chū)]
v. recognize, identify
e.g., 好久没见了，我一下子都没认出她来。

② 脱（下）[tuō(xià)]
v. take off
e.g., 他觉得热，就脱下了外衣。

好好在自己的房间里坐着，不要出门，更不应该穿成这个样子！"

但是，<u>祝英台</u>不仅觉得自己没有错，而且还对父母说出了自己的想法①。她说："爸爸妈妈，我想到<u>杭州</u>去读书。我可以穿男孩子的衣服，打扮成男孩子的样子，这样就没有人知道我是个女孩子了。你看，刚才连你们都没有认出我来，别人就更认不出来了。你们放心吧，我一定不会让别人认出来的，你们就让我去吧！"

父亲说："从来就没有女孩子出去上学的，就是打扮成男的，在外面生活也有很多不方便的地方。"

可是英台一定要去，父亲也没有办法，只好同意了。

　　母亲不放心女儿一个人出去读书，怕外面有坏人，要她带上丫环银心，还一次又一次地跟银心说，叫她一定要好好照顾①小姐。

6

① 挑 (tiāo) v.
carry something on
the shoulder
e.g., 他挑着两个箱子
在前面走，我跟在后
面。

② 书箱 (shūxiāng)
n. book box
e.g., 他的书箱里装
满了书，所以很重。

③ 亭子 (tíngzi)
n. pavilion
e.g., 公园里有很多亭
子，累了可以在那儿
休息一下。

④ 互相 (hùxiāng)
adv. each other
e.g., 我们班的同学都
互相关心，互相帮助。

第二天一大早，英台就带着丫环银心出发了。英台穿上男人的衣服，看上去就好像一个真正的男生。丫环银心打扮成书童，挑①着书箱②，跟在英台后面，两人一起离开家，高高兴兴地前往杭州去上学。

她们走了一会儿，觉得累了，就来到路边的一个小亭子③里休息。这时，路上走来一个书生和一个书童，他们也觉得累了，也想到亭子里来休息一下。英台跟这位书生互相④问了好，才知道他名叫梁山伯，也是去杭州上学的，他的书童名叫四九。他们四个谈得很高兴，于是，梁山伯和祝英台就在亭子里结拜①成了兄弟②。梁山伯比祝英台大两岁，所以祝英台就叫梁山伯"山伯哥哥"，梁山伯叫祝英台"英台弟弟"。梁山伯的书童四九也很喜欢祝英台的丫环银心，所以他们也学着主人③的样子，结拜成兄弟，然后

① 结拜 (jiébài)
v. become sworn brothers or sisters
e.g., 她们俩一见面就结拜成了姐妹。

② 兄弟 (xiōngdì)
n. brothers
e.g., 他俩是好兄弟，总是互相帮助。

③ 主人 (zhǔrén)
n. master, host
e.g., 他在这一家做工，主人对他很好。

① 同 (tóng)
adj. same
e.g., 我们是同一个
老师教的学生。

② 课桌 (kèzhuō) *n.*
desk, (school) table
e.g., 麦克和玛丽在
同一张课桌上学习。

③ 亲（弟弟）[qīn
(dìdi)] *adj.* blood/
biological (younger
brother)
e.g., 他们是同一个
母亲生的，是亲兄
弟。

他们就有说有笑地一起上
路了。

　　梁山伯和祝英台来到
学校，见了老师。老师看
到这两位聪明的少年来上
学，心里非常高兴。

　　老师让他们两个在同①
一张课桌②上学习。梁山
伯对祝英台就像对自己的
亲③弟弟一样，非常关心和
照顾；祝英台也很喜欢她

的山伯哥哥。祝英台觉得，梁山伯学习好，人也很好，她想，要是能跟这么好的人天天在一起，一定能学到很多东西，也一定会很快乐的！所以他们两个人从早到晚都在一起，互相关心，互相帮助，成了最好的朋友。

祝英台和梁山伯两人不仅白天在同一张课桌上学习，晚上还在同一个房间里睡觉。英台和丫环银心、山伯和书童四九，他们四个住在一个房间里。英台的床①和山伯的床互相挨着②，祝英台为了不让梁山伯发现她是个女的，就把两个书箱放在两人的床中间，书箱上还放上满满

① 床 (chuáng)
n. bed
e.g., 这张床很大，可以睡两个人。

② 挨（着）[āi(zhe)]
v. be next to, be close to
e.g., 小女孩儿总是挨着妈妈坐着。

① 盆 (pén) n.
basin, pot
e.g., 盆里装着水。

② 洒 (sǎ) v.
sprinkle, spill
e.g., 盆里的水太满
就容易洒出来。

③ 罚 (fá) v.
punish, penalize
e.g., 如果你做错了，
我们就罚你。

④ 师母 (shīmǔ) n.
the wife of one's
teacher or master
e.g., 我的老师和师
母都对我很好。

一盆① 水，她对梁山伯说：
"你睡觉的时候，一
定不要动，如果让盆里的
水洒② 了，我马上去告诉老
师，让他罚③ 你！"

梁山伯听了她的话，
睡觉的时候，真的一动也不
敢动。所以，梁山伯一直没
有发现祝英台是个女孩子。

可是祝英台打扮成男
人的事，早就被师母④ 看出

来了。师母把<u>祝英台</u>叫到跟前，问她是不是女孩子，<u>祝英台</u>只好跟<u>师母</u>说了真话。说完以后，她请师母一定不要告诉老师，更不要告诉其他的同学。师母是一个心地善良^①的女人，而且她自己也觉得，女孩子不应该每天关在家里，也应该出来学习读书写字。师母不仅同意不告诉别人，而且从那以后，她对这个聪明的女孩子更关心了。<u>祝英台</u>不管有什么心事，都来跟师母说，<u>师母</u>也像对自己的女儿一样爱她、关心她。

时间过得真快啊，<u>梁山伯</u>和<u>祝英台</u>已经在学校学习了三年了。这一天，

① 心地善良 (xīndì shànliáng) good-natured, kind-hearted e.g., 我的妈妈心地善良，总爱帮助别人。

12

① 收 (到) [shōu (dào)] *v.* receive
e.g., 她每个星期都能收到妈妈的信。

② 告别 (gàobié) *v.* bid farewell to
e.g., 他就要回国了，今天来跟我们告别。

祝英台收①到家里的信，说她的母亲病了，要她马上回家去。

祝英台向老师请了假以后，就过来找师母。她跟师母说，她和梁山伯已经在一起学习和生活了三年，她觉得梁山伯对她非常好，学习也很努力，她已经从心里爱上他了。跟师母告别②的时候，英台

交①给师母一把扇子②，扇子上画着一对漂亮的蝴蝶③，她说："等我走后，请您把这个交给山伯哥哥，让他去我家提亲④。"

祝英台就要离开学校了，她去跟梁山伯告别。听说他的"英台弟弟"要回家去，梁山伯心里很难过。祝英台走的那天，梁山伯送她下山，一直送了

① 交（给）[jiāo(gěi)]
v. hand over, deliver
e.g., 请同学们把作业交给老师。

② 扇子 (shànzi)
n. fan
e.g., 天气太热了，你有扇子没有？

③ 蝴蝶 (húdié)
n. butterfly
e.g., 我看到一只蝴蝶在那儿飞。

④ 提亲 (tíqīn) *v.*
propose a marriage
e.g., 他喜欢这个姑娘，就请了一个媒人去她家提亲。

① 河 (hé) *n.* river
e.g., 奶奶家门前有
一条河。

② 鹅 (é) *n.* goose
e.g., 河里有很多白
色的鹅。

③ 指（着）[zhǐ(zhe)]
v. point to, point at
e.g., 老师指着黑板
上的字问我们认不
认识。

④ 游 (yóu) *v.* swim
e.g., 我看到一只鹅
在水里游。

⑤ 母 (mǔ)
adj. female
e.g., 这只母鸡今天
生了一个鸡蛋。

很远的路。他们两人一路
上说着话，总是不愿意分
手。祝英台很想对梁山伯
说出自己的爱情，告诉他
自己是个女孩子，但又不
好意思说，只好想别的办
法来告诉他。

　　他们走着走着，看到
河①里有两只鹅②，祝英台就
指③着那两只鹅，对梁山伯
说："山伯哥哥，你看，河
里游④着两只鹅，母⑤鹅在

前面游，公①鹅在后面笑呵呵②。"

　　老实③的梁山伯没有听懂她的意思，还是往前走。祝英台开玩笑说："你真是一只呆头鹅④！"

　　又走了一会儿，他们看见路上有两只鸡，祝英台又指着那两只鸡对梁山伯说："山伯哥哥，前面有两只鸡，母鸡在前面走，公鸡在后

① 公 (gōng)
adj. male
e.g., 公鸡是不会生蛋的。

② 笑呵呵 (xiàohēhē)
adj. cheerful
e.g., 她很少生气，总是笑呵呵的。

③ 老实 (lǎoshi) *adj.*
honest, naive
e.g., 这个年轻人很老实，你不要跟他开玩笑了。

④ 呆头鹅 (dāitóu'é)
n. leatherhead
e.g., 他有些傻里傻气，大家都叫他呆头鹅。

① 笑嘻嘻 (xiàoxīxī)
adj. smiling cheerfully
e.g., 好好听我说，
别总在那儿笑嘻嘻
的。

② 大雁 (dàyàn) *n.*
wild goose
e.g., 你看，天上有
一只大雁在飞。

面笑嘻嘻①。"梁山伯听了，
还是不明白她的意思。

　　他们再往前走，看见
天上飞着两只大雁②，祝英
台又指着那两只大雁，跟
梁山伯说："山伯哥哥，你
看天上有两只雁儿在飞，
一个东来一个西，雁儿雁
儿听我说，你们最好不分
离！"梁山伯听了，还是

没明白。

　　他们又走了一会儿，
看见水里游着一对鸳鸯①，
祝英台又对梁山伯说："山
伯哥哥，你看那对鸳鸯，
它们游到哪儿都在一起！
如果我是女的，你愿意让
我做你的妻子，跟我永远
不分离吗？"

① 鸳鸯 (yuānyāng)
n. mandarin duck, a
symbol of lovers
e.g., 你看水里的那
对鸳鸯，多漂亮!

梁山伯说："可是你不是女的啊！英台弟弟，我们都快要分别了，我心里很难过，你怎么还总是鹅呀、鸡呀、鸳鸯呀地说个不停啊？你的心里就不感到难过吗？我真不明白你的意思！"

祝英台见梁山伯还是不明白，只好说："山伯哥哥，咱们两个人同学三年，你一直都很照顾我、关心我，你对我真是太好了，我很感谢你！现在我们就要分别了，我有一些重要的话要告诉你。你不是还没有结婚吗？我家里有个小九妹，长得跟我一样，我回去以后跟我父母说说，让他们把我的小九妹给你

做妻子，你愿意吗？不过，
你一定要记住早点儿到我
家里去提亲啊，就在七月
七日这一天去吧，一定不
要忘了啊！"

　　梁山伯本来就很喜欢
祝英台，听说她的妹妹跟
她长得一样，就高兴地说：

"好极了！七月七日我一定
会到你家里去提亲的！"

这时，前面出现了一
条大河，梁山伯不能再送
了，他们只好在这儿分手。
祝英台再一次跟梁山伯说：
"山伯哥哥，你一定不要忘
了早点儿去我家提亲啊！"
说完，就和银心上船去了。
梁山伯站在河边，望着祝

英台坐的船越走越远，心里非常难过。

祝英台回到家里，发现母亲并没有生病，父亲只是为了让她回家，才这么说的。一回到家，父亲就让祝英台换成女孩子的衣服，不让她再外出读书了。

这时正好有一家姓马的有钱人来提亲，父亲就同意了，准备让祝英台跟马家的儿子马文才结婚。可是祝英台说什么都不愿意，她对父亲说："我在杭州读书时，认识了一个同学叫梁山伯，他对我非常好，我已经爱上他了，我想跟他结婚。"

父亲一听，非常生气，

① 做主 (zuòzhǔ) v.
decide, take the
responsibility for a
decision
e.g., 我不知道该怎么
办，还是你给我做主
吧。

② 礼物 (lǐwù) n.
gift, present
e.g., 我姐姐要结婚了，
我想送她一件礼物。

他说："结婚这样的大事从来都是由父母做主①的，女孩子自己在外面找男人，像什么话？"父亲收了马家的礼物②，选好了日子，准备叫英台早点儿结婚。

送走祝英台以后，梁山伯又回到学校去读书。他虽然常常想着祝英台，想去祝英台家提亲，但他想到祝英台家很有钱，而自己家很穷，祝英台的父母怎么会看上他呢？就这样，日子一天一天地过去，七月七日到了。梁山伯心情很不好，不知道该不该去祝英台家提亲。

这一天，师母拿着扇子过来找梁山伯，跟他说了祝英台请她做的事，这时梁山伯才知道，祝英台

原来是个女孩子，她说的小九妹就是她自己！于是他马上向老师请了假，准备到祝家去提亲。一想到马上就能见到他的英台妹妹，梁山伯心里真是说不出的高兴。

梁山伯来到祝英台家里，告诉她家里的人，他是英台的同学，想跟英台见面。可是，他左等右等，也不见英台出来见他。过了好一会儿，才看见英台从她的房间里出来了。她穿着女孩子的衣服，样子更漂亮了。梁山伯马上走上前去，告诉英台说，他今天是来提亲的。可没想到祝英台一听这话，马上就大哭起来。她说："我的山伯哥哥啊，我走的时候不是跟你说，要你早点儿来吗？你为什么不早点儿来呢？你来得太晚了！我现在已经不可能跟你结婚了！"

梁山伯以为祝英台是因为他来晚了，生他的气，所以他还像以前他们在一起读书的时候那样，用大哥哥的口气跟她说："英台妹妹，这次真的是我错了，我太对不起你了！你要是生气，就打我吧！但是千万不要说这么叫我难过的话，我一定要跟你结婚，让你做我最漂亮的新娘①。"

祝英台一听，心里更难过了，她一边哭一边说："山伯哥哥，我说不可能跟

① 新娘 (xīnniáng)
n. bride
e.g., 中国人结婚的时候，新娘都穿红色的衣服。

26

你结婚，不是因为我生你的气了，而是因为我的父亲已经收了马家的礼物，我很快就要成为马家的人了，你现在来见我又有什么用呢？"

梁山伯一听，难过得说不出话来，两人都大哭起来。最后，他们哭着说："如果活着不能在一起，死了也决不分离！"

梁山伯回到家里，难过极了，也没有办法再去学校上学了。他太想祝英台了，想得吃不下饭，睡不着觉，没过几天就病倒了。他病得越来越重，他妈妈给他请了好几个大夫，吃了好多药，但都没有用。几天以后，梁山伯就病死了。快死的时候，他对家里的人说："我死了以后，你们

① 埋 (mái) *v.* bury
e.g., 他父亲死了以后，就埋在后面的山上。

② 抬 (tái) *v.* lift up, carry
e.g., 这张桌子太重了，帮我抬一下好吗？

③ 花轿 (huājiào) *n.* bride's sedan
e.g., 中国古时候，新娘都是要坐花轿的。

④ 吹吹打打 (chuīchuīdǎdǎ) *v.* beat drums and blow trumpets
e.g., 外面吹吹打打，有什么喜事吗？

⑤ 热闹 (rènao) *adj.* lively, bustling with noise and excite-ment
e.g., 春节到了，街上很热闹。

⑥ 闹 (nào) *v.* make a noise, cry or scream
e.g., 孩子总是闹着要出去玩儿。

一定要把我埋①在从祝家到马家的大路旁边，我要在那儿等着我的英台妹妹！"

过了几天，祝英台和马文才结婚的日子到了，马家的人抬②着花轿③，高高兴兴地来了。花轿停到祝家门口，吹吹打打④非常热闹⑤。可是祝英台却穿着白衣服，哭着闹⑥着，怎么也不愿意上花轿。父亲叫人给英台穿上新娘的衣服，

29

把她推①进花轿里，让马家的人抬走了。

　　但是，花轿抬到半路上，忽然起了大风，抬花轿的人都走不动了。这时丫环银心告诉祝英台，前面就是梁山伯的坟墓②。祝英台听了，就对抬花轿的人说："请你们停一下，我要到我山伯哥哥的坟墓前去跟他告别。如果你们不停下来让我去，我就自己跳下花轿去。"

　　抬花轿的人没有办法，只好停下花轿，让祝英台走下去，跟梁山伯告别。

　　祝英台来到梁山伯的坟墓前，脱下外面的新娘衣服，现出里面穿着的白衣服，放声大哭。她这一

① 推 (tuī) v. push
e.g., 门没锁，我推了一下就开了。

② 坟墓 (fénmù) n. grave, tomb
e.g., 这个坟墓里埋着两个人：丈夫和妻子。

30

哭，天地都被她感动了，
刚才还是晴天，现在却下
起大雨来了。

　　而且，不一会儿，让
人想不到的事情就发生了：
梁山伯的坟墓忽然打开了，
祝英台一边叫着"山伯哥
哥"，一边就跳进坟墓里去
了。旁边的人想去拉她，
可是已经太晚了。一会儿，

那打开的坟墓就又合①上了。马家请人来挖②，没想到挖开一看，里面什么都没有——梁山伯和祝英台两人都不见了。

人们很想知道，梁山伯和祝英台去哪儿了呢？就在这时，大家忽然看到两只漂亮的蝴蝶从坟墓里飞了出来。

① 合(上)[hé(shàng)] v. close
e.g., 请同学们合上书，我们现在开始听写。

② 挖 (wā) v. dig, scoop
e.g., 他在地上挖了个洞，把东西放了进去。

雨停了，风也住了，太阳又出来了。人们发现，这两只蝴蝶正在阳光下高兴地跳着舞呢，好像在告诉人们，它们感到非常的幸福！

　　看到这两只漂亮的蝴蝶，大家都说，它们一定是梁山伯和祝英台变的，他们说好要永远在一起，

现在他们终于在一起了！他们活着的时候，因为<u>祝英台</u>的父亲不同意，所以没能结成婚；现在他们死了，就变成了一对漂亮的蝴蝶，在天地间飞来飞去，永远地生活在了一起——从那以后，再也没有人能把他们分开了！

Butterfly Lovers

Long ago, there was a wealthy man whose family name was Zhu. People addressed him as Squire Zhu. He had a daughter, Zhu Yingtai, who was both beautiful and intelligent. She loved reading and writing. However, back in that time, girls were forbidden to seek an education at school, so Yingtai would sit by her window and look at the students passing by. Her mind wanted to fly out of the window to join them.

She wondered why girls had to stay in the house. Why couldn't she go to school? She called Yinxin, her servant girl, over. The two of them came up with a good idea—she would dress up as a man and go to school in a place far from home.

On that very day, Yingtai dressed up as a man and Yinxin dressed up as a servant boy. The two of them went to see Yingtai's parents. Her parents were having tea at the hall, then they saw a man and his servant boy approached and addressed them. They quickly rose and asked the man's name.

Yingtai was very glad that her parents didn't recognize her through her disguise. She took off the man's clothes and the other disguise. She addressed her parents again. They were surprised to see their own daughter. Her father said angrily, "A girl should behave like a girl—staying in her own room! A girl shouldn't step out of the gate, not to mention dress like this!"

However, Yingtai didn't agree with her father. She told her parents what was on her mind. She said, "Dad, Mom, I want to study in Hangzhou. I can wear men's clothes and act like a man. No one would know I'm a woman. Just now, you didn't recognize me, let alone strangers. Please rest assured. People won't see through my disguise. Please let me go!"

Her father replied, "It has never been heard of for a woman to go to school. Sure, you can dress as a man, but you will meet lots of problems living this way." However, Yingtai insisted on going. Her father couldn't convince her otherwise and had to give his consent.

Her mother was concerned if Yingtai went to school by herself, she might meet people with evil intentions. She asked Yingtai to take Yinxin with her. She told Yixin time and again to take good care of Yingtai.

Early the next morning, Yingtai set off with Yinxin, the servant girl. Yingtai looked like a man in men's clothing. Yinxin dressed up as a servant boy and carried the book box for Yingtai. Yingtai walked ahead and Yinxin followed her. The two of them left home and went happily on their journey to Hangzhou.

They felt tired after some hiking and rested in a pavilion by the side of the road. A student and his servant boy were also heading in the same direction. Feeling tired, they went to rest at the pavilion as well. Yintai and the student greeted each other. Yintai learned the student was Liang Shanbo who was also on his way to school in Hangzhou. Liang's servant boy was named Sijiu. The four of them had a nice conversation. So Liang and Yingtai took an oath of brotherhood. As Liang was two years older than Yingtai, she called Liang "older brother" and Liang called her "little brother." Sijiu, Liang's servant boy also felt an affinity for

Yinxin. And the two followed suit of their masters and became sworn brothers. After that, they happily continued their journey together.

Liang and Yingtai reached school and met their teacher. Their teacher was happy to see two brilliant young men joining him.

The teacher made Liang and Yingtai deskmates. Liang treated Yingtai as his own brother. He gave her a lot of attention and help. Yingtai also liked Liang since he was a kind person and excelled in his study. She considered it a joyful experience to be with such a nice person and learn from him every day! The two spent every day together. They cared for each other and helped each other. Naturally they became best friends.

Yingtai and Liang shared a desk during the day and one room during the night. The four of them, including Yinxin and Sijiu, lived in one room. Yingtai's bed was next to Liang's. Hiding from him the fact that she was a woman, she put two book boxes between them and a bowl full of water on top of them. She said to Liang,

"Don't move when you're asleep. If you touch the bowl and the water spills, I will tell the teacher and ask him to punish you!"

Liang listened to her and didn't dare to move a bit when he was in bed. So, he didn't discover that she was actually a woman.

The wife of their teacher noticed that Yingtai was a woman dressed up as a man almost immediately. She asked Yingtai to see her and asked if this was true. Yingtai had to tell her the truth. The teacher's wife was a very kind woman who also believed that girls shouldn't be confined to their homes and they should be allowed to study. The teacher's wife agreed to keep the secret for her. Moreover, she gave more attention and care to the clever young lady. When Yingtai was met with something that bothered her, she would go and talk to the teacher's wife, who treated her like her own daughter.

Time flew by and it had been three years since Liang and Yingtai started to study at school. One day, Yingtai received a letter from home. The letter said that her mother was ill and she was expected to return home immediately.

Yingtai asked her teacher for leave, then she went to see the teacher's wife and told her that for three years she had studied with Liang and lived together with him; she thought that Liang was very nice to her and he studied diligently, so she fell in love with him. When she bade farewell to the teacher's wife, Yingtai gave her a fan on which a beautiful pair of butterflies were drawn. Yingtai said, "After I'm gone, please pass it to Liang and ask him to come to my home to propose."

As Yingtai was about to leave school, she went to say goodbye to Liang. He was upset when he learned that his "brother" was leaving for home. On the day she departed, Liang accompanied her on her long trip down to the foot of the mountain. They talked and walked. Both of them were reluctant to part with each other. She wanted to tell Liang her feelings for him, to tell him that she was a woman, but she was too shy to confess that. Therefore, Yingtai tried to make hints.

As they were walking down the mountain, they saw two geese in the river. Pointing at the geese, Yingtai said to Liang, "Brother, take a look, two geese are swimming in the river: the female goose swimming ahead while the male one is following happily after her."

Simple-minded, Liang didn't get her hint and continued to walk. Yingtai made fun of him by saying, "What a stupid goose you are!"

After a while, they saw two chickens walking. Yingtai again pointed at them and said to Liang, "Brother, there are two chickens before us. The hen is walking ahead while the rooster is walking joyfully after her." Liang heard her words, but didn't understand what she wanted to say.

They went further and saw two wild geese in the sky. Yingtai pointed at them and said to Liang, "Brother, look, two wild geese are flying in the sky. One is to the east and one is to the west. I want to tell the wild geese that I wish they would never part from each other!" Still, Liang didn't get her hint.

After some time, they saw a pair of mandarin ducks, a symbol of lovers, in the water. Yingtai said to Liang, "Brother, see that pair of mandarin ducks? They swim together everywhere. If I were a woman, would you like to take me as your wife and never part with me?"

Liang said, "But you're not a woman. Brother Yingtai, we are going to part and I'm very upset about that. Why did you go on and on talking about the geese, chickens and mandarin ducks? Don't you feel sad right now? I don't know what is going on in your mind!"

Realizing Liang didn't get her hints at all, Yingtai had to say, "Brother Liang, we have been classmates for three years, during which you took very good care of me. You've been very kind to me and I appreciate that. Now that I'm leaving, I have something very important to tell you. I know you're not married. I have a little sister who resembles me. I want to be the matchmaker and ask my parents' permission to marry her to you. Are you willing to take her as your wife? But do remember to come to my home to propose to her in a timely manner. July 7th seems to be a good day. Propose to her on that day. Bear this in mind!"

Liang was fond of Yingtai. When he learned Yingtai and his sister were similar, he gladly agreed, "Great! I will go to your home and propose to her on July 7th!"

A big river was ahead and Liang couldn't accompany Yingtai any further. They had to part here. Yingtai once again said to Liang, "Brother Liang, don't forget to go to my home soon to propose!" With that, she boarded the ship with her servant girl. Standing by the river, Liang was overcome with sadness as he watched the boat carrying Yingtai fade into the distance.

Yingtai returned home and found her mother was well. Her father just needed an excuse to make her return home. Upon returning home, her father asked her to change into a woman's dress and forbade her from going to school.

Then, the wealthy Ma family came to propose a marriage alliance. Yingtai's father gave his consent and planned to marry Yingtai to Ma Wencai. Yingtai certainly would not agree to that. She said to her father, "When I was studying in Hangzhou, I met Liang Shanbo, a classmate. He has been very nice to me and I fell in love with him. I want to marry him."

Her father was furious upon hearing this. He said, "Big decisions such as marriage should be left to the parents. What a shame if a girl finds herself a husband!" Her father accepted the gift from Ma's family and picked their wedding day. He wanted Yingtai to get married soon.

For Liang Shanbo, he returned to school and continued his study after he saw Yingtai off. Often, he would think about Yingtai. He wanted to propose a marriage to the Zhu family, but given that he came from a humble family, how could he find favor in their eyes? Days passed and it was already July 7th. Liang felt quite distressed as he was hesitant about the marriage proposal.

The teacher's wife brought a fan to Liang and told him what Yingtai asked her to do. Liang came to know that Yingtai was a woman in disguise and her little sister was herself! He wasted no time asking leave from his teacher and was going to propose to Zhu's family. The thought of seeing Yingtai again delighted Liang.

Liang went to Zhu's family. He told them he was Yingtai's classmate and wanted to meet her. However, he waited for a long time to see Yingtai walking out from her room. She looked more beautiful in a woman's dress. Liang approached her and told her he planned to propose to her this very day. To his surprise, Yingtai started to weep. She said, "Brother Liang, upon my departure I told you to come to my home earlier. Why didn't you come early? It's too late! Now it is impossible for me to marry you."

He thought she was simply blaming him for being late. So like in the old days, he tried to comfort her like a big brother. He said to Yingtai, "Sister Yingtai, it's my fault. I'm so sorry. If you want, you can beat me to let your anger out! But please don't say such cruel things. I will definitely marry you and you will be the most beautiful bride."

Yingtai felt even more heartbroken upon hearing this. She wept, "Brother Liang, I told you I can't marry you, not because I'm angry with you, but because my father has accepted a marital gift from Ma's family, the family I'm marrying into. Your coming to see me won't change anything."

Knowing that, Liang felt so heartbroken that words failed him. The two of them cried together. Finally, they said with tears, "If we can't be together in real life, may death join us together!"

Liang returned home. He was too upset to go to school. He missed Yingtai so much that he could neither eat nor sleep. He became sick after a couple of days and his condition became worse and worse. His mother found several doctors for him and they gave him plenty of medicine. Unfortunately, none of them helped. Several days later, Liang died of his illness. On his deathbed, Liang said to his family, "After I die, please bury me by the road connecting Ma's and Zhu's families. I will wait for Sister Yingtai there!"

After a few days, the wedding of Yingtai and Ma took place. Carrying the bride's sedan, the Ma family came to pick up Yingtai. It was a joyful occasion for them. The sedan stopped at the gate of Zhu's family. Various instruments were being played for this occasion. However, Yingtai dressed in white instead of the traditional bridal red. She was weeping and struggling to stay out of the sedan. Her father demanded her to wear the bridal dress and forced her into the sedan. Then Ma's family carried the sedan away.

However, on their way, a strong wind rose. People carrying the sedan couldn't move ahead. Yinxin, the servant girl, told Yingtai that Liang's tomb lied ahead. Knowing that, Yingtai said to the porters carrying the sedan, "Please stop here. I want to say goodbye to Brother Liang in front of his tomb. If you refuse, I would jump out of the sedan anyway."

The porters had to stop the sedan and allow Yingtai to step out and bid farewell to Liang.

Yingtai walked to Liang's tomb. She took off her bridal dress and revealed the white dress underneath. She began to wail. The heaven and earth were moved by her. So the sun gave way to a heavy rain.

After a while, something even more mysterious happened. Liang's tomb cracked open and Yingtai threw herself into it while crying, "Brother Liang!" Those who stood beside her tried to pull her out but failed. In a split second, the crack in the tomb closed. Ma's family sent people to open the tomb, but only to find it was empty—both Yingtai and Liang had disappeared.

People were wondering where Liang and Yingtai went, then they saw two beautiful butterflies fly out of the tomb.

The rain stopped, the wind ceased, and the sun appeared. People found the two butterflies were dancing joyfully under the sun. They seemed to tell the crowd that they were truly happy.

People saw the two beautiful butterflies and believed that they were transformed from Liang and Yingtai. The two lovers promised to be together forever. In this way they kept their promise! When they were alive, they didn't get the chance to be married because Yingtai's father refused to give his consent. In death, they became a pair of beautiful butterflies flying freely between the heaven and the earth. They would live together forever as no one could ever separate them!

练习题 Reading exercises

1. 梁山伯跟祝英台是什么关系？（　　）

　　A. 父女　　　B. 兄妹　　　C. 兄弟　　　D. 恋人

2. 祝英台的丫环名字叫什么？（　　）

　　A. 四九　　　B. 很心　　　C. 银心　　　D. 狠心

3. 英台把自己打扮成一个男子，把丫环打扮成什么？（　　）

　　A. 老师　　　B. 书童　　　C. 员外　　　D. 书生

4. 看到打扮成男人的英台，她的父母一开始怎么样？（　　）

　　A. 没有认出来　　　　　B. 认出来了

　　C. 很高兴　　　　　　　D. 想到了

5. 英台想打扮成男人去哪里上学？（　　）

　　A. 上海　　　B. 杭州　　　C. 广州　　　D. 梅州

6. 祝英台和梁山伯是在哪儿结拜成兄弟的？（　　）

　　A. 学校里　　B. 家里　　C. 亭子里　　D. 大树下

7. 英台在学校里学习了几年？（　　）

　　A. 一年　　　B. 两年　　　C. 三年　　　D. 四年

8. 祝英台和梁山伯的床中间放着什么东西？（　　）

　　A. 两把椅子　B. 两个书柜　C. 两张桌子　D. 两个书箱

44

9. 书箱上还放了什么？（　　　）

　　A. 一盆花　　　　　　B. 一盆水

　　C. 一个杯子　　　　　D. 一个瓶子

10. 祝英台回家以前，交给师母一个什么东西？（　　　）

　　A. 一把扇子　　　　　B. 一条手绢

　　C. 一幅画儿　　　　　D. 两只蝴蝶

二、判断题：请根据故事内容判断下列说法是否正确，如果正确请标"T"，不正确请标"F"。
Decide whether the following statements are true (T) or false (F).

1. 祝英台的父亲名叫"祝员外"。　　　　　　　（　　　）

2. 祝英台的丫环名叫"银心"。　　　　　　　　（　　　）

3. 男扮女装去外地上学这个主意是祝英台和丫环一起想出来的。　　　　　　　　　　　　　　　（　　　）

4. 祝英台比梁山伯大两岁。　　　　　　　　　（　　　）

5. 梁山伯和祝英台在学校里是同桌，也是同屋。（　　　）

6. 师母很关心祝英台，像对自己的女儿一样爱她。（　　　）

7. 三年以后，祝英台的母亲生病了，她父亲叫她回去。（　　　）

8. 祝英台有一个妹妹，跟她长得一模一样。　　（　　　）

9. 祝英台的父亲觉得女孩子不应该自己找男人。（　　　）

10. 梁山伯和祝英台死了以后，变成了两只蝴蝶。   (   )

1.从前有个（   ）祝的有钱人，大家都（   ）他祝员外，他有一个女儿叫祝英台。祝英台不仅（   ）得漂亮，而且还很聪明。她很（   ）读书写字，但是那时候，女孩子是不能出去上学读书的。英台每天站在自己房间的窗户旁边，望着外面（   ）的读书人，她的心早就（   ）出去了。

A. 飞   B. 长   C. 姓

D. 喜欢   E. 叫   F. 来来往往

2.老师让他们两个在同一张（   ）上学习。梁山伯对祝英台就像对自己的亲（   ）一样，非常关心和照顾；祝英台也很喜欢她的山伯（   ）。祝英台觉得，梁山伯学习好，人也很好，她想，要是能跟这么好的人天天在一起，一定能学到很多东西，也一定会很快乐的！所以他们两个人从（   ）到（   ）都在一起，互相关心，互相帮助，成了最好的（   ）。

A. 晚   B. 弟弟   C. 课桌

D. 早   E. 朋友   F. 哥哥

3. 一个多月（　　）了，有一天，师母（　　）着扇子过来（　　）梁山伯，跟他说了祝英台请她做的事，这时梁山伯才（　　），祝英台原来是个女孩子，她说的小九妹就是她自己！于是他马上向老师（　　）了假，准备到祝家去（　　）。

A. 找　　　　B. 过去　　　　C. 拿

D. 提亲　　　E. 请　　　　　F. 知道

4. 梁山伯回（　　）家里，难过（　　）了，也没有办法再去学校上学了。他太想祝英台了，想得吃不（　　）饭，睡不（　　）觉，没过几天就病（　　）了。他病得越来越重，他妈妈给他请了好几个大夫，吃了好多药，但都没有用。几天以后，梁山伯就病（　　）了。

A. 死　　　　B. 下　　　　C. 到

D. 极　　　　E. 着　　　　F. 倒

5. 看到这两只漂亮的蝴蝶，大家（　　）说，它们（　　）是梁山伯和祝英台变的，他们说好要（　　）在一起，现在他们（　　）在一起了！他们活着的时候，因为祝英台的父亲不同意，所以没能结成婚;（　　）他们死了,就变成了一对漂亮的蝴蝶，在天地间飞来飞去，永远地生活在了一起——从那以后，（　　）没有人能把他们分开了！

A. 现在　　　B. 都　　　　C. 再也

D. 永远　　　E. 一定　　　F. 终于

1. 请根据故事内容连线，组成完整的句子。

A. 祝英台不仅长得漂亮　　　a. 心里非常高兴

B. 英台把丫环银心叫过来　　b. 现在他们终于在一
　　　　　　　　　　　　　　　起了

C. 英台看到父母都没有认
　　出她来　　　　　　　　c. 而且还很聪明

D. 他们两个人互相关心、　　d. 一起想出了一个好
　　互相帮助　　　　　　　　　办法

E. 他们说好要永远在一起　　e. 成了最好的朋友

2. 根据故事内容为下列事物选择各自的特征。

A. 梁山伯　　　　　a. 心地善良的

B. 祝英台　　　　　b. 满满的

C. 师母　　　　　　c. 像呆头鹅一样的

D. 读书人　　　　　d. 聪明漂亮的

E. 一盆水　　　　　e. 来来往往的

A. 梁山伯和祝英台结拜成兄弟。

B. 祝英台告诉梁山伯，她有个跟她长得一样的妹妹，让梁山伯七月七日去她家提亲。

C. 祝英台女扮男装去杭州上学。

D. 祝英台收到家里的信，说她的母亲病了，要她马上回家去。

E. 祝英台跳进了梁山伯的坟墓，从坟墓中飞出了两只漂亮的蝴蝶。

F. 梁山伯后来病死了。快死的时候，他让家里人把他埋在从祝家到马家的大路旁边。

G. 祝英台回家后，她的父亲收了马家的礼物，准备把她嫁给马家。

H. 梁山伯来到祝英台家里，两人大哭起来。

六、图片题。 Answer the following questions according to the picture.

1. 图片中有几个人？他们是谁？

2. 图片中的人在哪儿？他们在干什么？

3. 图片中的两个人是谁？你觉得她们在说什么？

4. 图片中的两个人是谁？他们为什么哭？

52

练习题答案 **Keys to the exercises**

一、选择题
　　1. D　　2. C　　3. B　　4. A　　5. B
　　6. C　　7. C　　8. D　　9. B　　10. A

二、判断题：请根据故事内容判断下列说法是否正确，
　　如果正确请标 "T"，不正确请标 "F"
　　1. F　　2. T　　3. T　　4. F　　5. T
　　6. T　　7. F　　8. F　　9. T　　10. T

三、选择填空
　　1. C　　E　　B　　D　　F　　A
　　2. C　　B　　F　　D　　A　　E
　　3. B　　C　　A　　F　　E　　D
　　4. C　　D　　B　　E　　F　　A
　　5. B　　E　　D　　F　　A　　C

四、连线题
　　1. A-c, B-d, C-a, D-e, E-b
　　2. A-c, B-d, C-a, D-e, E-b

五、请根据故事内容给下列句子排列顺序
　　C-A-D-B-G-H-F-E

词汇表
Vocabulary List

挨（着）	v.	āi(zhe)	be next to, be close to
办法	n.	bànfǎ	method, means, way
窗户	n.	chuānghu	window
床	n.	chuáng	bed
吹吹打打	v.	chuīchuīdǎdǎ	beat drums and blow trumpets
聪明	adj.	cōngmíng	clever, intelligent
打扮	v.	dǎban	dress up, make up
大厅	n.	dàtīng	hall, lobby
呆头鹅	n.	dāitóu'é	leatherhead
鹅	n.	é	goose
罚	v.	fá	punish, penalize
坟墓	n.	fénmù	grave, tomb
告别	v.	gàobié	bid farewell to
公	adj.	gōng	male
合（上）	v.	hé(shàng)	close
河	n.	hé	river
蝴蝶	n.	húdié	butterfly
互相	adv.	hùxiāng	each other
花轿	n.	huājiào	bride's sedan
交（给）	v.	jiāo(gěi)	hand over, deliver
结拜	v.	jiébài	become sworn brothers or sisters
课桌	n.	kèzhuō	desk, (school) table
老实	adj.	lǎoshi	honest, naive
礼物	n.	lǐwù	gift, present
埋	v.	mái	bury
母	adj.	mǔ	female
闹	v.	nào	make a noise, cry or scream
盆	n.	pén	basin, pot
亲（弟弟）	adj.	qīn(dìdi)	blood/biological (younger brother)

热闹	*adj.*	rènao	lively, bustling with noise and excitement
认（出）	*v.*	rèn(chū)	recognize, identify
洒	*v.*	sǎ	sprinkle, spill
扇子	*n.*	shànzi	fan
师母	*n.*	shīmǔ	the wife of one's teacher or master
收（到）	*v.*	shōu(dào)	receive
书童	*n.*	shūtóng	servant boy attending to study
书箱	*n.*	shūxiāng	book box
抬	*v.*	tái	lift up, carry
提亲	*v.*	tíqīn	propose a marriage
挑	*v.*	tiāo	carry … on the shoulder
亭子	*n.*	tíngzi	pavilion
同	*adj.*	tóng	same
推	*v.*	tuī	push
脱（下）	*v.*	tuō(xià)	take off
挖	*v.*	wā	dig, scoop
想法	*n.*	xiǎngfa	idea, thought
笑呵呵	*adj.*	xiàohēhē	smiling cheerfully
笑嘻嘻	*adj.*	xiàoxīxī	joyful, smiling
心地善良		xīndì shànliáng	good-natured, kind-hearted
新娘	*n.*	xīnniáng	bride
兄弟	*n.*	xiōngdì	brothers
丫环	*n.*	yāhuan	maid, servant girl
雁	*n.*	yàn	wild goose
游	*v.*	yóu	swim
鸳鸯	*n.*	yuānyang	mandarin duck, a symbol of lovers
照顾	*v.*	zhàogù	look after, care for
指（着）	*v.*	zhǐ(zhe)	point to, point at
主人	*n.*	zhǔrén	master, host
做主	*v.*	zuòzhǔ	decide, take the responsibility for a decision

项目策划：刘小琳　韩　颖
责任编辑：刘小琳
英文翻译：张　乐
英文编辑：薛彧威
英文审订：黄长奇
封面设计：E·T创意工作室

图书在版编目（CIP）数据

梁山伯与祝英台：汉、英／王亚西改编．——北京：华
语教学出版社，2016
（"彩虹桥"汉语分级读物．2级：500词）
ISBN 978-7-5138-0975-7

Ⅰ．①梁… Ⅱ．①王… Ⅲ．①汉语－对外汉语教学－
语言读物 Ⅳ．① H195.5

中国版本图书馆CIP数据核字（2015）第155705号

梁山伯与祝英台

王亚西　改编

*

©华语教学出版社有限责任公司
华语教学出版社有限责任公司出版
（中国北京百万庄大街24号　邮政编码 100037）
电话：(86)10-68320585　68997826
传真：(86)10-68997826　68326333
网址：www.sinolingua.com.cn
电子信箱：hyjx@sinolingua.com.cn
新浪微博地址：http://weibo.com/sinolinguavip
北京玺诚印务有限公司印刷
2016年（32开）第1版
2017年第1版第2次印刷
（汉英）
ISBN 978-7-5138-0975-7
定价：15.00元